WRITE NOW

JAIME MUNT

MUNT

WRITE NOW

The prompts in this book are based on fiction. Names, characters, organizations, places, events, and incidents are either products of the author's imagination or are used fictitiously. Any resemblance to actual persons, living or dead, businesses, companies, events or locales is entirely coincidental.

Published by Jaime Munt

Photography courtesy of Pixabay.com

ISBN-13: 978-0692630792
ISBN-10: 0692630791

Printed in the United States of America

CONTENTS

IMPORTANT: PLEASE READ

People buying this book for the young writer in their life might consider censoring the section "DARK and DIRTY" which encourages people to brave that kind of writing in a meaningful and artistic way. The prompts themselves might invoke images inappropriate for some ages. Please review this section before giving this book to people under 18 years of age.

MUNT

WRITE NOW

JAIME MUNT

HOW THIS WORKS

Writing is a game where you set all the rules. Edgar Allen Poe coined more than three-hundred-and-fifty words. Cormac McCarthy doesn't follow punctuation rules as were iron-fistedly enforced in grammar school and English classes, because to him they aren't necessary—and he's an utterly brilliant writer!

In writing you can make your own world and completely ignore scientific law and logic— because *you* say it is so.

This makes our options of what to write about as vast as the cosmos, so then why is it that we sometimes have such a hard time thinking of something to write about?

The aim of this book is to try and help with that. Hopefully it will encourage the development of regular writing habits, expand the reach of your imagination, and give you a ready answer to the horrible conundrum of what to write about.

Writing every day is the only way to work up your writing muscles—unless you're just that talented, which would be grossly unfair—but the rest of us need practice.

SUGGESTIONS for MAKING the MOST OUT of WRITING PROMPTS

✎ 🗎 ✎

* Start cold – take in just what the prompt says and WRITE! Don't think, just do it!

- or –

* Warm up to the prompt, get some ideas first and see where they take you.

* In general, I limit a prompt to three-five minutes of writing as constantly as I can make myself.

- but –

*DO challenge yourself! Do ten and thirty minute writing challenges. Don't rule out one hour endurance challenges.

* THINK BROAD – prompts are just there to fuel your brain. If a prompt about oranges gets you writing about mummies, RUN WITH IT! That's not breaking any rules, but perhaps reaching the exact point where these exercises are supposed to help take you – TOTAL IMAGINATIVE FREEDOM!

* WHEN YOU'RE DONE? Come up with your own prompts! Challenge friends – see how differently you each interpret them.

*MOST IMPORTANTLY….

Enjoy yourself.

SENSES and EMOTIONS

Sometimes it's hard to convey a feeling or thought. Hopefully this section will help you develop the way you express these things in writing.

- ☐ Describe love lost.

- ☐ Describe someone's clothing: think about smell, texture, brand, color, etc.

- ☐ Write about or describe someone dealing with or accepting guilt.

- ☐ Write about or describe someone falling.

- ☐ Write about someone reacting to their reflection.

- ☐ Write about or describe someone being stubborn.

- ☐ Write about or describe someone trying not to cry.

- ☐ Write about someone awakened in the night.

- ☐ Write about or describe someone ill.

- ☐ Write about someone reflecting on their life.

- ☐ Write about or describe someone cooking.

- ☐ Describe a nightmare.

- ☐ Write about or describe someone trying not to lose their temper.

- ☐ Write about or describe someone grooming.

- ☐ Write about someone pressed for time.

- ☐ Write about fear.

- ☐ Write about being lost.

- ☐ Write about or describe someone drunk.

- ☐ Describe eating an apple.

- ☐ Write about or describe a dance/dancing.

- ☐ Describe or write about being cheated on.

- ☐ Describe or write about a child coping with "the boogeyman".

- ☐ Describe love at first sight.

- ☐ Describe eating something wonderful.

- ☐ Write about or describe putting on jewelry or makeup.

- ☐ Write about no longer fitting into your favorite pair of jeans.

- ☐ Describe a sneeze.

- ☐ Write about envy.

- ☐ Write about or describe eating.

- ☐ Describe the confession of something awful.

- ☐ Describe the scent of a perfume.

- ☐ Write about or describe waking up cold.

- ☐ Write about or describe a toothache.

- ☐ Write about someone betrayed.

- ☐ Write about people or person having fun.

- ☐ Write about or describe a child.

- ☐ Write about someone who is not normal, imagining about how things would be if they were.

☐ Write about someone suddenly realizing their power or weakness.

☐ Write about someone becoming a parent or finding out they will be.

☐ Write about someone disgusting or doing disgusting things.

☐ Describe someone's discomfort at being really hot or cold.

☐ Write about or describe someone stubbing a toe, bumping into something hard, scraping their knee, etc.

☐ Write about or describe someone with allergies.

☐ Write about or describe a heart attack.

NATURE

How do we make a reader lose themself in your story, part of that is by fleshing out your scenes with lots of "props and special effects".

Imagine you are a set builder, you know where you want your characters to be, what is the weather, the mood you want to convey—so think about what you would ask your effects and prop people to buy, if you have it on your list, don't you think you should mention it to your readers?

- ☐ Write about or describe winter.

- ☐ Write about or describe perfect, peaceful weather.

- ☐ Write about or describe a bar.

- ☐ Write about or describe spring.

- ☐ Write about or describe a "creepy place".

- ☐ Write about or describe summer.

- ☐ Write about or describe a school.

- ☐ Write about or describe a setting that invokes a sense of awe.

- ☐ Write about or describe fall.

- ☐ Write about or describe fire.

- ☐ Write about or describe a prison or jail.

- ☐ Write about or describe dirt or rocks.

- ☐ Describe a burial or grave.

- ☐ Write about or describe water.

- ☐ Focus on time of day.

- ☐ Describe a grocery store.

- ☐ Write about or describe air

- ☐ Describe a forest scene.

- ☐ Write about or describe a severe storm.

- ☐ Write about or describe a mechanic's shop.

- ☐ Describe a holiday or festival.

- ☐ Write about or describe night.

- ☐ Write about or describe paradise.

- ☐ Describe a library.

- ☐ Describe a region or landmark.

- ☐ Describe a disgusting or clean bathroom.

- ☐ Write about someone almost drowning or choking.

- ☐ Write about or describe a road or path.

- ☐ Describe "Home".

- ☐ Write about or describe the sounds of being in nature.

- ☐ Write about or describe the sounds of being out on the town.

- ☐ Describe a dazzling sunrise or sunset.

- ☐ Describe being outside after a rain.

- ☐ Write about or describe a camping scene.

- ☐ Write about or describe dirty clothes.

- ☐ Describe a creepy alley.

- ☐ Imagine working in a mine.

- ☐ Write about or describe someone having a relaxing bath.

- ☐ Write about or describe someone in the middle seat on a long plane ride.

- ☐ Write about someone running into an ex while with their new partner.

- ☐ Write about being worried.

- ☐ Write about or describe being shocked with cold water.

30 minute FREE WRITE – GO!

REALITY CHECK

The following section of writing prompts focuses on autobiographical writing. While the purpose of prompts is to kick start your writing engine and these can certainly be approached fictionally, these exercises are geared toward non-fiction writing, memoirs, etcetera, etcetera...

Just the same, good fiction has to be believable. Someone famous once said fiction has to make more sense than non-fiction – so writing about your own thoughts and experiences can be good practice.

- ☐ Write about the best dream you can remember

- ☐ Write about your favorite holiday and why.

- ☐ Write about or describe your favorite childhood toy.

- ☐ Write about or describe your dream man or woman.

- ☐ Write about or describe your ideal date.

- ☐ Write about or describe a "sanctuary" or hiding place.

- ☐ Write about or describe first love.

- ☐ Write about or describe your worst date.

- ☐ Write about the worst nightmare you've ever had.

- ☐ Write about or describe someone who's an inspiration to you.

- ☐ Write about or describe your dream life.

- ☐ Write about the worst thing you've ever done.

- ☐ Write about where you think or plan to be in 5 or 10 years.

- ☐ Write about best memory of school.

- ☐ Write about or describe your dream job.

- ☐ Write about or describe your first experience with death.

- ☐ Write about your best childhood memory.

- [ ] Write about the scariest thing that has ever happened to you.

- [ ] Write about feeling insecure.

- [ ] Write about or describe your worst childhood memory.

- [ ] Write about or describe your greatest fear.

- [ ] Write about getting older.

- [ ] Write about or describe your funniest memory.

- [ ] Write about or describe childhood friends.

- [ ] Write about childhood or youthful antics.

- [ ] Write about the first time you ever broke the law.

☐ Write about the best night you ever had out with friends.

☐ Write about or describe a childhood friend who you've forgotten or haven't spoken to in years.

☐ Write about being by yourself or feeling lonely.

☐ Write about or describe your favorite food. Why?

☐ Write about your first pet.

☐ Write about or describe something that scared you as a child which you regard as ridiculous now.

☐ Write about your favorite subject in school.

- [ ] Write about or describe witnessing someone being treated badly. How did you feel?

- [ ] Write about a family vacation or trip.

- [ ] Write about or describe your first day of school.

- [ ] Write about or describe your favorite relative.

- [ ] What you regret most.

- [ ] Write about a mentor/confidant.

- [ ] What's the meanest thing you can remember doing?

- [ ] Write about or describe what religion's meant in your life.

- [ ] Write about or describe siblings or not having them.

- ☐ Write about or describe your first paying job.

- ☐ Write about someone who annoys the heck out of you.

- ☐ Write about someone who intrigues or interests you whom you've never spoken to.

- ☐ Write about someone you idolized in youth.

- ☐ Write about popularity.

- ☐ What's the most amazing thing you've ever experienced?

- ☐ What's the bravest thing you've ever done?

- ☐ What's the stupidest thing you've ever done?

SWORDS, SORCERY, and SCI-FI

I love fantasy! As a pure escapist, even into the realms of horror, I enjoy the freedom fantasy writing gives me. I name my own planets, countries, kingdoms, laws, dangers and the reach of magical capabilities. In some worlds, magic is a rare and almost unheard of gift, while in others magic is rampant and the most powerful among them liken themselves to deities! Have some fun with this section – here, you make ALL the rules.

Exert your Deus ex Machina!

- ☐ Write about powerful creatures battling each other.

- ☐ Describe a very un-earthlike world.

- ☐ Write about or describe a battle between technology and magic.

- ☐ Write about or describe a warrior.

- ☐ Write about or describe a magician.

- ☐ Write about or describe an archer.

- ☐ Write about or describe someone's apprentice.

- ☐ Write about or describe a falconer.

- ☐ Write about or describe a knight.

- ☐ Write about or describe someone of royalty.

- ☐ Write about a moment between a human and non-human.

- ☐ Describe someone or something undead.

- ☐ Write about or describe an android or cyborg.

- ☐ Write about someone or something abnormal.

- ☐ Write about or describe a spell being cast.

- ☐ Write about someone fighting a hopeless battle.

- ☐ Write about or describe a troll.

- ☐ Write about or describe a sci-fi weapon.

- ☐ Write about someone overcoming insurmountable odds.

- ☐ Write about or describe a futuristic space station.

- ☐ Write from the point of view of the family or spouse of an adventurer.

- ☐ Write about or describe the tension before a battle.

- ☐ Write about or describe a ghost or spirit.

- ☐ Write about team of villains against one hero and/or vice versa.

- ☐ Write about someone meeting a race for the first time.

- ☐ Write about or describe a space craft.

- ☐ Describe an unnatural or unearthly object.

- ☐ Write about or describe a marketplace.

- ☐ Describe a new world.

- ☐ Write about or describe a vampire.

- ☐ Write about or describe someone or something shapeshifting.

- ☐ Write about a person who goes to the beach one morning to find the water has turned blood red.

- ☐ Write about a hero who turns evil or someone evils who turns good.

- ☐ Write about or describe a creature exploring sand.

- ☐ Describe and name a magical weapon.

- ☐ Describe a brand new race.

- ☐ Write about someone when they discover they have superpowers.

- ☐ Describe a hostile alien.

- ☐ Write about or describe an alien abduction.

- ☐ Write about or describe a futuristic or fantasy city.

- ☐ Write about or describe a futuristic means of transport.

- ☐ Write about or describe a highway robbery by bandits.

- ☐ Describe a dragon's lair.

- ☐ Write about or describe a mythical beast attacking people or a place.

- ☐ What if people lived underwater?

- ☐ Write about a post-apocalyptic word.

- ☐ Describe someone's gear.

- ☐ What lurks in that mountain fortress?

- ☐ Write about an encounter with an ancient being.

- ☐ Write about someone finding out they're immortal.

- ☐ Write about "unlikely companions".

- ☐ Write about or describe a villain.

- [ ] Write about or describe bizarre weather.

- [ ] Write about an immortal dying.

- [ ] Write about or describe a gladiator.

- [ ] Write about or describe a potion.

- [ ] Write about or describe a leprechaun.

- [ ] Write about someone returning from battle.

- [ ] Write how the thief got in there.

- [ ] Write about or describe a siege.

- [ ] Write about or describe a futuristic police force or criminals.

- [ ] Write about or describe time travel.

30 minute FREE WRITE – GO!

DRAW FROM WHAT YOU KNOW

The prompts in this section encourage you to make something more of the ordinary and assert the fact that inspiration is everywhere.

(Think about how it makes you feel, the story, the characters…)

- ☐ Think about a song you hate—
  now write your own story from it.

  (Think about how it makes you feel, the story, the characters…)

- ☐ Think about a song you love—
  now write your own story from it.

  (Think about how it makes you feel, the story, the characters…)

- ☐ Consider your nearest carpet or
  rug, imagine it is somewhere
  else. What is it present to witness
  or experience?

- ☐ Your razor could have a story,
  maybe it already does—tell it!

- ☐ A closet holds more than just
  clothes…

- ☐ Here are some household items
  that might deserve a little more
  thought or creative attention:

o car keys

o ash tray

o washing machine

o butter knife

o that sock with no partner

o the morning paper

o your curtains or blinds

o maybe a hidden door behind your wallpaper…

□ What is your drive or walk home like?

□ What are you most afraid of?

□ Look around the room – stop on the first thing that catches your eye—now imagine a world where that suddenly doesn't exist.

- ☐ Hold out your arms—whatever is within arms' reach is all your character has with them when marooned on an island, in the woods, or stranded in their car during a snow storm.

- ☐ Turn off anything in the room that makes sound, if you can, and write what's passing through your walls, or maybe what could be…

- ☐ You look at or out your window, but it is a view of somewhere else.

- ☐ You are trapped in your house— by what, why, and what will you do???

- ☐ You look to one side and find a strange creature belly-crawling up beside you or your feet.

PURE FICTION

In this section I've tried to bring together prompts that provoke events, situations, interactions—scenes!

ACTION!

☐ Write about someone getting memory back after amnesia, for example.

☐ Write about someone who has done something another person has accepted the blame for.

☐ Waking in the night to a loud crash!

☐ Write about or describe someone being rude or childish.

☐ Write about someone saving someone.

☐ Write about or describe someone riding something.

☐ Write about someone doing something for the first time.

☐ Write about or describe someone performing an art.

- ☐ Write about someone being confronted about an issue regarding their health.

- ☐ Write about a person or people's reaching to a night that lasts long into the next afternoon.

- ☐ Write about someone trying to earn or renew another person's respect.

- ☐ Write about a midwife who goes to the aid of a mother and what she hopes will be an uneventful birth.

- ☐ Write about a brief encounter with a stranger that changes a person's life.

- ☐ Write about someone, who by fault of their own, cause someone they care about to be injured.

- ☐ Write about someone who is invited to join a bizarre religious meeting, i.e. cults or perhaps snake handlers.

- ☐ Write about someone who, when walking down the street, see a pair of glowing eyes peering out of a sewer drain.

- ☐ Write about a blind woman's guide dog who begins to speak with her when they're alone.

- ☐ Write about being alone in the house and clearly hearing walking or running inside.

- ☐ Write about someone dealing with a bad customer.

- ☐ Write a "pick up" scene.

- ☐ Write about someone who returns from a trip or errand claiming to have met the devil or like entity.

- ☐ Write about someone who claims to be an emissary of God after surviving a disaster against all odds.

- ☐ Write about a person in an asylum who's trying to convince their shrink their paranoia/hallucinations are real.

- ☐ Write about someone's reaction to their best friend telling them a horrible secret.

- ☐ Write about a woman who buys a gun for self-defense, but a few days later can't find it.

- ☐ Write about or describe overhearing a conversation, between two people you've never met, that shocks or disturbs you.

- ☐ Write about someone placing a food order at a restaurant or drive-thru.

- ☐ Write about someone experiencing a life or developmental milestone.

- ☐ Write about or describe a moment of complete selflessness or selfishness.

- ☐ Someone just lost their job and now they have to tell their spouse.

- ☐ Daycare or babysitter called, the child is missing!

- ☐ Write about someone and their animal companion.

- ☐ Write about someone being discriminated against.

- ☐ Write about someone being captured or arrested.

- ☐ Consider and interaction between a veteran and a youth.

- ☐ Write about or describe a mercy killing.

- ☐ Write an interrogation.

- ☐ Write about a grand ball or a dance.

- ☐ An "undesirable" attends a social event.

SINGLE WORD PROMPTS

Never underestimate the power of a word. The right word can make the difference between whether you respond with, "Oh?" or "OH!" Even words that mean essentially the same things can invoke different emotional responses. Go on your gut and see what happens when you let ONE WORD invoke something in you.

- ☐ HATE

- ☐ PATIENCE

- ☐ APPLICATION

- ☐ TERMINATION

- ☐ RESERVATION

- ☐ LOSER

- ☐ SLIVER

- ☐ GRAY

- ☐ HOT

- ☐ SLOBBER

- ☐ PIRATE

- ☐ CRAVING

- ☐ HEIRLOOM

- ☐ SOUL

- ☐ MIGRAINE
- ☐ SURGERY
- ☐ CARAMEL
- ☐ COLD
- ☐ CREEP
- ☐ WEATHERED
- ☐ MOON
- ☐ RICH
- ☐ CRUNCH
- ☐ DIVE
- ☐ JOKE
- ☐ WEAK
- ☐ MYTHOLOGICAL
- ☐ CUT

- ☐ DISASTER
- ☐ MARBLE
- ☐ SOGGY
- ☐ POWERFUL
- ☐ POOR
- ☐ HEAVY
- ☐ SHOCK
- ☐ TOLL
- ☐ MUSHROOM
- ☐ BEAUTIFUL
- ☐ FOG
- ☐ BLACK
- ☐ JOHN
- ☐ TEAR

- ☐ SILK
- ☐ MAROONED
- ☐ UGLY
- ☐ LIGHT
- ☐ PROUD
- ☐ ALIEN
- ☐ PEEVE
- ☐ BOSS
- ☐ HABIT
- ☐ BINOCULAR
- ☐ LAWN
- ☐ RAVEN
- ☐ RED
- ☐ SHAME

- ☐ TRAFFIC

- ☐ FUR

- ☐ HONOR

- ☐ TALL

- ☐ BLIND

- ☐ HYPNOSIS

- ☐ OBLIGATION

- ☐ RAT

- ☐ STRANGER

- ☐ IDLE

- ☐ INCIDENT

- ☐ TEXT

- ☐ IDOL

- ☐ BABY

1 PAGE FREE WRITE – GO!

EXAGGERATING or ELABORATING

It's easy to misunderstand what someone wants or feels in emails and letters, because when we read things we project a tone and it might not even be in the same universe as what the writer was actually intending.

Luckily, when we talk to people, most the time, we don't have the same trouble explaining or expressing ourselves. The people in our stories aren't so lucky.

If I write "Hey!" Do you read someone reacting in alarm or do you read a happy greeting? I'm curious about what backstories you'll read into these prompts.

61

Here is some dialog that you might have fun twisting, taking on face value, or stretching into creative lengths where others might exclaim:

"How in the world did you go from that to this?"

- "The only thing I've got left is my pride"

- "I can't believe you let him drive…"

- "After everything he's done, you're still going to…"

- "I knew it was wrong, but they threatened to fire me."

- Please don't take this the wrong way, but I have to tell you something that's been bothering me.

- "Your life isn't worth a damn to me."

- "Look what I found in the dumpster."

- "You know I hate it when you…"

- ☐ Write a prompt based on this sentence: "How'm I supposed to go to the bathroom?"

- ☐ "Death, to me…"

- ☐ "I ran farther and farther every day, but I never did get out of that town. Not really…"

- ☐ "I looked down, and that's when I saw it…"

- ☐ "Personally, I think they're a cult"

- ☐ "Sometimes when I dream it feels like there's someone else in there with me."

- ☐ "Um, I think you broke it."

- ☐ "How did you get in here?"

- ☐ "You might notice a foul odor"

- □ "This is all I have."

- □ "I can't believe you said that!"

- □ "I'm here about the ad in the paper..."

- □ "How could anyone ignore it?"

- □ "I'm conducting a study..."

- □ "Are you following me?"

- □ He was born that way, I guess...

- □ "How do I look?"

- □ "You smell terrible, what happened?"

- □ "I had to have it..."

- □ "You're a long way from home, boy."

☐ "I know you're not religious, but why don't you try praying anyway."

☐ "Where on earth did you find that?"

☐ "I know it's terrible, but I kind of like hurting people."

☐ "Don't pretend to know what I'm going through."

☐ "That homeless guy is staring at you again."

☐ "Whatever you do, don't turn on the light, please."

☐ "No one can predict when there life is about to change…"

☐ "Don't look at me like that."

☐ "So where are you from?"

- ☐ "What's that noise?"

- ☐ "So what do you do around here?"

- ☐ "I wasn't trying to stare, it's just that she's beautiful, don't you think?"

- ☐ "I want my money back."

- ☐ "We can't let this continue."

- ☐ "Forgive me father, for I have sinned, a lot."

- ☐ "Do what I tell you and everything will be just fine."

- ☐ "What do you intend to do with that?"

- ☐ "A haunted what?"

- ☐ "I'm not who you think I am..."

☐ "What did you say?"

☐ "My parents always said my imaginary friend would go away when I got older… it didn't."

☐ "And that's when I quit."

☐ "Served him right."

☐ "Funny how your eyes always look away when you say that."

☐ "Don't worry. I believe you."

☐ "If you could accuse someone of being downright evil, it would be him."

☐ "He was pretty religious once…"

☐ "Look, somebody's got to make a decision."

☐ "I just had the weirdest dream about you."

- ☐ "You never know what you can do, until you do it.

- ☐ "They invented a word for guys like him."

- ☐ "The end justifies the means…"

- ☐ "…never going to do that again."

- ☐ "Stop thinking about how much you love them, start thinking about how much they hurt you."

- ☐ "Don't!"

- ☐ "Do you ever think you could go through with it?"

- ☐ "I think I survived pretty good actually. You should have seen everyone else."

- ☐ "I can't believe you don't remember me."

☐ "That's my cue to leave the room…"

☐ "When I was a little kid, I always…"

☐ "If misery loves company, there are none more social than I…"

☐ "Let's try that again…"

☐ "I would have been here, but…"

☐ "Today I saw someone who looked just like you. You won't believe what they were doing…"

☐ "I may never get another chance to tell you…"

☐ "I never thought he'd have the guts to show his face…"

☐ "Hey!"

☐ "Another second in there and I'd have lost my mind…"

☐ "That was when I realized I wasn't like everyone else…"

☐ "I don't care what you or anyone else says. I don't believe in…"

☐ "As I stood there, absorbing my new surroundings, I started to wonder if I was better off…"

☐ "Are you sure this is a short cut?"

☐ "I ate. What other choice did I have?"

☐ "Nobody understands what I went through…"

☐ "You're probably wondering what I'm doing on this ledge…"

PICTURE PROMPTS

If someone were to look at the pictures you take, what stories or feelings would they provoke? Would they look at the child sitting on the sidewalk and think, 'That looks so sad and lonely.' When the truth was that the child had just finished a tantrum from hell and was sulking.

If I lay a pen out on the table in front of you, does it have a story sleeping inside it? Can it? Yes! Nothing is simple in the mind of a writer. Nothing ever has to be mundane.

MUNT

MUNT

MUNT

MUNT

MUNT

MUNT

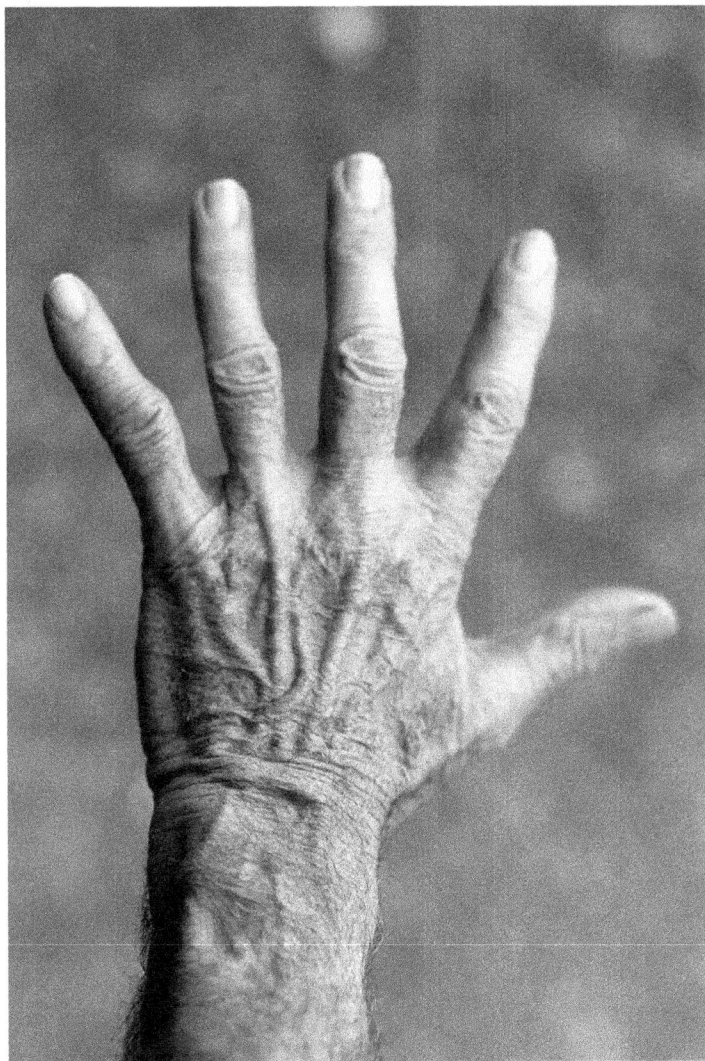

MUNT

MUNT

MUNT

MUNT

MUNT

MUNT

MUNT

MUNT

MUNT

MUNT

MUNT

MUNT

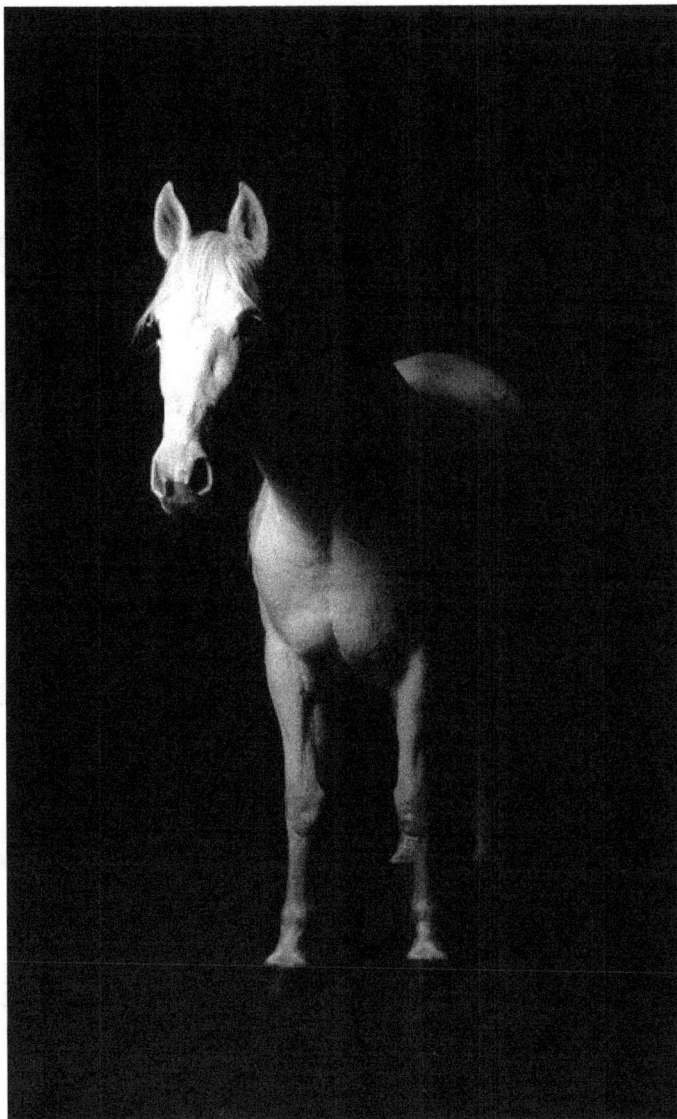

DARK and DIRTY

⬿▤⬾

Not everything in books is suitable for children or even teenagers—obviously! But, for some of us, leaving the safety of PG writing is really hard to do. We don't want our parents, friends, co-workers to read how well we can describe a murder or a steamy sex scene. Some writers take it too far and are shocking in a forced, purposeful way. Readers can't always swallow the dark and dirty stuff in huge doses.

This section of prompts is supposed to help you become comfortable with writing the tough stuff or help you polish the grit, you already love to write, and turn even the most repulsive death scene into prose with a purpose and creative conscience that your readers will ache when reading instead of losing their lunch.

Some of these prompts should not be attempted by people under 18 as they may conjure images inappropriate for people of that age.

- ☐ Write about someone receiving a fatal injury.

- ☐ Write about someone obsessing about someone/something.

- ☐ Write about cannibalism.

- ☐ Write about or describe a seedy hangout for criminals.

- ☐ Write about an adult or parent's worst fear.

- ☐ Describe an adult goods store.

- ☐ Write about or describe a funeral.

- ☐ Write about or describe romantic lovemaking.

- ☐ Write about or describe being burned alive.

- ☐ Write about or describe giving birth.

□ Write about someone getting vengeance.

□ Write about or describe someone dealing with a progressive and unignorable physical problem – like skin falling off or parts of the body keep moving around (like finding your mouth on the bottom of your foot).

□ Write about or describe broken bones.

□ Write about waking to find someone in your room.

□ Write about or describe bad sex.

□ Write about patricide or matricide.

□ Write about someone literally cursed.

- ☐ Write or describe a crime scene.

- ☐ Write about someone who knows they will or is about to be eaten alive by an animal or something else…

- ☐ Write about someone being beaten or beaten up.

- ☐ Write about vomit or someone throwing up.

- ☐ Imagine coming out of the shower and finding someone just entering your bathroom.

- ☐ Describe someone naked.

- ☐ Swear, a lot, and give it a purpose!

- ☐ Write about or describe dismemberment.

- ☐ Write about or describe suffocation.

- ☐ Describe someone's body odor.

- ☐ Write about or describe a close encounter battle or gang fight.

- ☐ Write about or describe pulling teeth.

- ☐ Write about someone being mugged.

- ☐ Write about or describe an apocalypse.

- ☐ Write about or describe something humiliating.

- ☐ Write about or describe an autopsy.

- ☐ Describe the worst monster you can think of.

- ☐ Describe the worst human being you can imagine.

- ☐ Write a bad ending.

- ☐ Write about or describe a plague.

- ☐ Write about someone getting a sliver or pulling one out.

- ☐ Describe the world's worst papercut.

- ☐ Describe someone coming home to find their family dead.

- ☐ Write about or describe a serial killer.

- ☐ What's the most painful thing that can happen to someone?

- ☐ Write about or describe a car accident.

- ☐ Write about someone bleeding and think "poignant".

- ☐ Write about or describe an adult club.

- ☐ Write about or describe someone doing drugs.

- ☐ Write about or describe some kind of abuse.

- ☐ Write about or describe someone's darkest fantasy or wish.

- ☐ Imagine Hell.

- ☐ Write about someone caught snitching on the worst possible person.

- ☐ Write about or describe torture.

30 minute FREE WRITE – GO!

PROMPT STEW

These are the prompts that I couldn't fit into neat little categories. These prompts run the gambit and hopefully will really get your creative juices going.

- ☐ Write about a vigilante or freedom fighter.

- ☐ Write about someone making an important choice toward their fate.

- ☐ Write about two people who are like night and day.

- ☐ Write about sacrifice.

- ☐ Write about or describe someone writing.

- ☐ Write about something being or already stolen.

- ☐ Write about a slumber party or child's first sleepover.

- ☐ Write about someone taking a test.

- ☐ Write about someone on the verge of fame or infamy.

- ☐ Write about or describe a sideshow or freak show.

- ☐ Write about someone with an unpleasant job.

- ☐ Write about someone realizing war is inevitable.

- ☐ Write about a ceremony or tradition.

- ☐ Write about someone and a comfort item.

- ☐ Write about a dinner with friends.

- ☐ Write about or describe a sport or game.

- ☐ Write about someone and their pet.

☐ Write about or describe a victory.

☐ Write about extinction.

☐ Describe a fight.

☐ Write about a precious item.

☐ Write about God or a god and His or its response to something.

☐ Write about or describe a person's reaction to a newborn that is physically abnormal.

☐ Write about someone who has devoted their life to religion, but begins to doubt the existence of God.

☐ Write about a waiter, clerk, or bartender who begins to have prophetic visions about the customers.

- ☐ Write about someone with nothing to lose, intent on challenging the best in their field to regain their pride.

- ☐ Write or describe a detective.

- ☐ Imagine getting into a pool and suddenly realizing there is a shark or huge alligator in it too.

- ☐ When the stranger sitting beside you leaves, you discover they left or forgot something with your name on it…

- ☐ Write about or describe a secret society.

- ☐ Write about or describe, literally, "What the cat dragged in".

- ☐ Write about or describe an After Life.

☐ Write about someone with a mental disorder or disability.

☐ Describe a face.

☐ Write about someone waking after having thought they were dead.

☐ Write about or describe someone being chased.

☐ Write about someone leaving reluctantly or being kicked out.

☐ Write about or describe a teacher.

☐ Write about someone making a big mistake.

☐ Write about a reward.

☐ Write about or describe a nursing home.

☐ Write a fan-fic about your favorite fictional character.

☐ Write about someone getting three wishes.

☐ Someone's mouthy parrot suddenly begins to spout predictions of the future.

☐ Someone waking up into someone else's body or life.

☐ Someone has just had the best day of their life, when the trend does a horrifying 180.

☐ Two unlikely people falling in love.

☐ Write about or describe the thoughts of animals as they watch us.

WRITE YOUR OWN PROMPTS

☐ _____

_____

☐ _____

_____

☐ _____

_____

☐ _____

_____

☐ _____

_____

☐ _____

_____

☐ _____

_____

☐ _____

_____

☐ _____

_____

☐ _____

_____

☐ _____

_____

☐ _____

_____

☐ _____

_____

☐ _____

_____

☐ _____

_____

☐ _____

_____

WRITE NOW

☐ _____

_____

☐ _____

_____

☐ _____

_____

☐ _____

_____

☐ _____

_____

☐ _____

_____

☐ _____

_____

☐ _____

_____

☐ _____

_____

☐ _____

_____

SO YOU MADE IT THROUGH

I've loved writing since I was four and my oldest brother started teaching me cursive –much to the chagrin of my elementary school teachers— should you see my penmanship now, you'd understand!

Doing writing prompts alone or with friends and family is something I've not only enjoyed but mentally *craved.*

Hopefully you've liked the writing exercises in this book and have even thought of your own.

On a side note: remember, the pleasure you get from writing is more important than the approval you do or don't get from the people who read it.

If you enjoy writing, don't let anyone discourage you. Not everyone likes the same thing. You're going to love something someone else hates and vice-versa.

If you're a small time writer, like me, try not to take reviews and ratings personally. I've learned a lot from criticisms that bother to explain what's working for them and what's not—that's valuable stuff, make it work for you.

Keep writing—GO!

ABOUT ME

Interest, not practicality, drove me to earn a Bachelor of Fine Arts Degree in Creative and Professional Writing. It has taken me awhile to do much of anything with it, beyond writing, writing, writing, every chance I get.

Now that I've independently authored about half a dozen books and published the works of several other authors, I'm finding a little satisfaction from this lifelong passion.

I don't foresee a day when my nine to five can be abandoned to do this full-time, but I'm always hoping… and scratching lottery tickets.

I wish you good luck in whatever you want to be or do.   Thanks for reading about me.

www.ingramcontent.com/pod-product-compliance
Lightning Source LLC
Chambersburg PA
CBHW071338290326
41933CB00039B/1370